I Don't Love You

CHRISTIAN WETHERED

I DON'T LOVE YOU

Goggles
EYEWEAR PAMPHLET SERIES 2018

First published in 2018
by Eyewear Publishing Ltd
Suite 333, 19-21 Crawford Street
Marylebone, London W1H 1PJ
United Kingdom

Typeset with graphic design by Edwin Smet
Author photo by Christian Wethered
Printed in England by Lightning Source
ISBN 978-1-912477-48-7

WWW.EYEWEARPUBLISHING.COM

TABLE OF CONTENTS

Goggles

PRESENT

In carpentry I made you a jewellery box.

The drawers have grooves for
Opening and closing on their wheels,
The flat bases covered
With velvet.

And when you close them they give
The tiniest thud.

To open the box takes a tug after which
It rolls back open.

I wonder where you'll put your necklace,
Your rings. The bottom drawer is
For pearls.

I hope you like it. Mr Barnhurst

Did most of the sawing.
The sanding was all me –

I used to rub so it went hot.
Mr Barnhurst was almost deaf
So it was hard to get his attention
In a crowd of boys.

He'd clamp it in
And saw the pieces down from a big block.
Sawdust clouded on our lips as we watched.

Goggles

PINK LADY

Cold from the
fridge
flesh
white hard
the incisor
splits skin
follows through
your
eyes widen
when the crunch
pulls
the slow chunk
shiny with beads
unclasping from
the root

LETHE

After Baudelaire

I like to lick the hole with my tongue,
listen to it melting, widen, soften.

When I kiss it will follow,
easing to muscle like a lip –

she lets you in; and once in, the space
is warm, dark, like the inside of a

mountain – invisible but such tenderness
there to stretch. It sucks you back

when you give, lets you in. Try the
whole hand if you like, the smell is

tipped with sugary sweat, something
luxurious and soapy. The inside is

an aroma you've never tried –
stale, yes; dark and ripe.

Goggles

SHEETS

When Helen folded them, such precision.
She let me stay on the mattress like a dog while she
settled sheets around, so slow
to lay down their hands on my back and ears, fold
to where I was, the contours of my back.

BEDTIME

Your shoulders pink from the shower
as you apply cream on cheeks,
smile, towel around your head.

Bending down to stretch,
your epilator pulling the roots from
thighs.

Sitting to pee as I brush my teeth,
you chat about a colleague,
breasts waving, as I spit and reply:

She's just jealous.

FEBRUARY

Even her hands are cold. I lift one
like a doctor. She is absent from me.
                          She looks
and thinks to the world with her eyes,
straying upward. She needs
to leave me now; she unfastens her hand.

BREAK

We'll discuss your things:
table, chairs, English notes,
the double mattress. I'll ask
how you are and eyes will prick.
I'll want to walk away but a tiny wire will keep me tight.
                              Casual as possible,
I'll ask if there's a chance.

SHE SAID

the blacks of your eyes are holes
where I feel cold
where breath will leave me inarticulate
as though you hold a mirror
the depth of my inadequacy
as you stare constant as stone
until I am nothing
and know you've won
and I won't return to you
wounded man in a child's face
who learned to hold me to your cold
so I was frightened and scattered away
and even as I breathe I struggle
to gather words

HE SAID

(i)

You let me scream
say terrible things
which is fine for a while
then I wish I wasn't so mean
your eyes like a child's
in a manager's suit
dusky from the train

(ii)

I sat you down
and screamed
just kept screaming
I didn't know what else to do
your blank eyes
what can you say to silence?
behind you weren't there
tortoise in your shell
outside eyes were fixed
I knew I'd hit on something
hard to define
beyond me
I wanted to save
you

Goggles

SINGLE

My parents are coming today, out of love.
They'll sit on my sofa,
drink tea; my mother will make
suggestions about decoration, colours;
my father will sit behind his mug
as I dart, sink.
We won't say much but I wonder what
they'll make of my Matisse: if it's crooked,
too small for the space;
whether I should have made the holes
in the walls.

COAST

sitting next to the sea
with scruffy hair blowing
reminds me of hairdryers
at school the massive ones
the matrons held while we
stood in a line waiting for
hot air to blow down our necks
our hardening towels
smelling of each other

Goggles

PULL

I met a boy he wasn't
attractive I needed to sleep
with him

it could have been nice to sleep
with him even though it was
just a mood I wanted to sleep
with him forever
I think he felt the same
maybe we should have slept
together

he wasn't very pretty
I think that's why I wanted him
I'm less attracted to
the attractive ones
the less attractive ones
are effortless

I want to sleep with this kind of boy
no one too beautiful or too much

someone with nice arms
kind eyes

PARK

calmer than I was a few
days agothe air
warmerandmy mind doesn't
stirlike beforedon't
care about things today sitting
on the grasswaiting

don't want the darkest thoughts
to circle firstI want to
divide
everything how itis

Goggles

TAXI

I shivered on the warm side
of the window, tracing the moon,
branches skittering past.

Then turning down the lane
It appeared the other side;
I shivered again,
though warm;
the loud heater sustaining us all –

man on the wheel; the rest of us
curled in different angles –
waiting

for the moon to close its eye
over everyone.

MICHAELMAS

Why give up
on a postcard, the sweetness of a postcard?
When I was at school I wouldn't look
up to see if I'd got a card, a letter.
So often it was the case – her squiggly love
at the top of the pile, a tiny face
on the envelope. Inside, paragraphs for me:
lines made perfect by her love.
The underlying thing was always love.
Daddy's were weekly, blue paper, gentle slant,
longer. I think about it now and I cry,
not because I was sad, but because I can still
remember a world I keep having to explain
as though it's not there, wasn't there.

NEW YEAR'S

The strange star at the end of the road
is ringing billions of years old now,
as you listen, only in the shadows;
and your light and body are already
gone – as far as the next star can tell;
but knowing this, you return home,
hang your coat on your peg and listen
to a girl humming; and you go to her,
cling around her shoulders and back,
her smile lifting as you stop thinking
of the inconceivable everything,
and take relief in the small things –
which are enough for one man,
with every second slipping.

ACKNOWLEDGEMENTS

With many thanks to the following publications for featuring my work: Poetry Ireland, The Moth, The Caterpillar, Brittle Star, Café Writers, Cinnamon Press and Aesthetica.

With particular thanks to Eve Grubin and Clare Pollard for their continued support and advice. Finally, thank you to Todd Swift at Eyewear, and to Rosanna Hildyard for her editorship.

Lightning Source UK Ltd.
Milton Keynes UK
UKHW012032151218
334088UK00001B/98/P